Earnest Poetica

Ink Expressions of the Ineffable Heart

By

Sati Siroda

Book Ecke

Earnest Poetica

Ink Expressions of the Ineffable Heart

By

Sati Siroda

Published by Book Ecke
15A, 4th Floor, City Vista, Tower A,
Suite No.1140, Fountain Road, Kharadi, Pune - 411014
Website: www.bookecke.com

ISBN
eBook: 978-81-966458-1-6
Paperback: 978-81-966458-4-7
Hardback: 978-81-966458-2-3

First edition [2023]
Visit www.bookecke.com for any further information.

To those who persist and do their best, this tribute stands…

BOOKS BY SATI SIRODA

Mind the Quote

Poulomi's Abode of Thoughts

Coffee Tales: Short Stories of Wisdom

Earnest Poetica: Ink Expressions of the Ineffable Heart

Gratitude Journal: Reflect, Appreciate, Transform in 60 Days

Inspiring Stories for Amazing Girls Who Believe in Themselves

Inspiring Stories for Amazing Boys Who Believe in Themselves

I Am 6 and Wonderful

I Am 6 and Brave

Author's Note

"Earnest Poetica" is a captivating collection of poems that dive deep into those big, complex emotions we all feel but sometimes can't seem to put into words. You know, those feelings that stir in your heart and swirl in your mind but get lost on the way to your lips.

Writing these poems, I realized how powerful words can be in capturing the essence of our human experiences—the joy, the pain, the whole rollercoaster. This isn't just a book; it's a journey through all those intense emotions we've all felt at some point.

I've poured my heart into these pages, hoping they resonate with you, offering a sense of connection, understanding, and maybe even a bit of comfort. So, if you've ever felt something deeply but struggled to express it, "Earnest Poetica" is for you.

Yours truly,

Sati

Table of Contents

Your Free Gift

Hey There, Seeker of Poetry and Wisdom!

Adulting comes with its highs and lows, but here's something to make your journey a little more exciting—**two** free e-books, just for you! Whether you need a spark of creativity, a dose of inspiration, or just a fresh perspective, these gifts are here to add a little extra spark to your day.

1. **You Got This- Mindful Reflections Journal**
   - Thoughtful prompts to enrich your reading journey
2. **Mandala Coloring Book**
   - A creative way to unwind and cultivate mindfulness

Scan Me

1. Indeed, a Man's Best Friend

Mixed or pure, short, or tall,

These little cuddles of joy have the hearts of all,

They are our little angels who guard us through,

They love, they hug, and they are souls, so true.

Life without a furry bundle,

Is a life that might grumble,

They are indeed a man's best friend,

A friend in need till life's end.

Not a day or two is enough to love and care,

A word or two to explain their presence is not enough to share,

They are pure love, purest of all,

And all they need is you, and that is all!

2. As You Grow Older

Amidst the darkest dawn and the brightest light,

There's a bond that is worth a sight,

Loveth is the nameth, and heart is where it stays,

"Liveth longeth," my soul prays.

As you grow older, the heart grows fonder,

Memories linger, and dreams ponder,

As the years pass by, with a wink of an eye,

The more I know you, the more I love you, and the more my heart wants to fly.

The approaching future and the shadows of the past,

May memories be made that a lifetime will long outlast.

As you inch towards your goal and age with grace,

May the bond grow strong, and together, we can ace.

3. The Lion

Larger than life, smarter and rife,

These look majestic and sharper than a knife.

With a golden sun-kissed body and a crown to match,

They seem lazy, but your dreams, they can snatch.

They prowl, they hunt, they growl, they grunt,

They leap, they sleep, they turn, they run.

In every action, there is life, and that life sounds lyrical,

With every reaction, they appear mystical.

Earnest Poetica

The female hunts, the male protects,

These big cats, too, have human reflex,

Funny! Isn't it... That when the lioness grunts,

Even the great male... shunts.

4. Tiger: "You Woke Me Up..."

As I slept in peace,

You woke me up in greed.

I rested my head in nature's lap,

You saw me, you liked, and aloud you clapped.

Every passer-by stood, took out their machines and clicked-clacked,

The sleep that had just ventured in went back.

More the dreaded look I gave,

You clicked more and thought it was brave.

All I wanted, for heaven's sake, was to rest,

But you thought, to click, this was the time that you gave your best.

Irritated and agitated, I got up and left,

You woke me up, and I call it a silent theft.

5. Dresden Frauenkirche, Saxony, Germany

At last, those clouds found a way,

Covering even the last gleaming sunshine ray,

The Kirche stood amidst the bustling crowd,

Showered love and peace on each passer-by, as it had vowed.

Spreading love even on the gloomiest day,

Is what a brave must do and thus carve their own way,

The lesson well taught by the architecture and passed upon,

Amidst the clouds, it is going to stand forever and on.

6. *Persian Leopard and Hope on a Snowy Day*

He walked, and he growled,

With every step in his aesthetic, I drowned,

He leapt in the snow and stood tall and majestic,

I cried with joy as he looked ever calm and magnetic.

I looked around, and nothing seemed furthermore comprehensive,

By now, the heart had settled its battle and was no more apprehensive,

The sycamore had aroused and brought back the soul,

Taught a lesson about fearlessness and its role.

The faith in nature and life on a snowy day was restored,

Just by looking at this feisty creation, positivity roared,

As it walked and twisted its tail, as it looked around,

Even on the deadliest winter day, a ray of hope was found.

This leopard taught us wearily life's magnum opus,

And rejected the idea of being hocus-pocus,

Sati Siroda

He led us to a visionary world and commanded for 'the faith,'

Though sometimes gloomy, life still sends up the smoke of hope's wraith.

7. Lake Öschinen, Switzerland

~ A Trail Towards Salvation

I walked the trail down to the lake,

Passing by the beautiful landscape,

My blood gushed into my veins like never before,

The idea of getting lost overpowered, therefore.

Yeah! The skies there leaned over the water, caressing it quietly,

I stood in amazement and watched the creation silently,

As I moved ahead, the trees embarked on its presence,

The winds felt cold and gusty as well as pleasant.

I walked and walked and then sat to rest,

That little bench at the centre is where I caught the nature at its best,

I looked around and couldn't stop mushing over,

My heart, already at this point, became a gushing rover.

Over the skies, with the wind, to the mountains, it flew,

Touched the snow, kissed the breeze, and bid it adieu,

On the way back, it stopped by to collect some drops of dew,

The memories it fetched are going to stay, it seems, forever and new.

8. *I'm a Woman.*

I'm a woman and can't be torn into two,

True that, I'm a woman, and it's true...!

I'm a woman, and my feelings aren't out of the blue,

My heart beats with strength, every beat anew.

I'm a woman, with strength and grace anew,

With a heart that beats for me and for you.

I'm a woman, with dreams and goals to pursue,

Breaking barriers and ceilings, nothing I can't do.

I’m a woman, with a voice that rings clear and true,

Demanding equality and respect, long overdue.

Yes, I’m a woman, and proud to be who,

I am, unapologetically, through and through.

For I am human, with emotions that, breakthrough,

A soul that seeks understanding, a heart that’s true.

I’m a woman with depth and complexity, too,

A mind that thinks, a spirit that soars, and a spirit that always grew.

My feelings may be strong, but that's not something new,

For I am a woman with passions that renew.

So let me be, let my emotions shine through,

For they're a part of who I am, and they're as valid as any hue.

9. Those Who Wish Me Dead

Even when people wish me dead,

On life's path, I tread,

I ain't easy to be dominated,

I am here to succeed, and I know I'm fated!

Those who wish me dead,

Must know that I am here to stay instead,

I ain't easy to be overpowered,

I am truly blessed and empowered!

Sati Siroda

While you're wishing me dead,

I am overcoming my failures instead,

With closed ears and eyes on the path,

I walk firmly towards success with another start!

10. The Unfilial Child

Beaten at a tender age,

The child knew why he was raised,

Mortified time and again,

Only abuse he gained!

Shackled and dusted with the pain,

He was just a means to monetary gain,

Bounded with responsibilities, he couldn't even bend,

He knew he was born to meet the expectations till the end.

When he couldn't bear it anymore,

He decided to swim across the shore,

With the label of being unfilial,

He stopped considering the matter trivial.

11. Never Take Life for Granted

When you see the sunshine and smile,

Know that darkness will come, and you mustn't whine,

When you see the clouds and fain,

Know that it will soon rain.

When you take life for granted,

Know that soon, things will become unwanted,

When you see the moon and crave,

Know that it won’t shine in the grave.

When you feign ignorance and trifle,

Know that soon, life is going to make you stifle,

When you learn from your mistakes,

Know that- that is when a smooth road life takes.

12. Latvia: A Baltic Crush

The sea, the rivers, the mountains, and the greens,

The eyes are captivated by the flowing streams,

Trees standing amidst the snow, mighty and tall,

Once again, in love, the heart is ready to fall.

The autumns and the springs have their stories to tell,

The mighty medieval architectures have their tales and smell,

Indeed, a hidden treasure of northern Europe,

In its presence, the serendipity is sure to gallop.

With miles to trek and nature to adore,

Latvia is sure to amuse you with its folklore,

It stands out as an enchantress of beauty,

Charming every visitor and considering that as its duty.

13. Nature Stays Pristine

Oceans are beautiful & serene,

Nature knows how to stay pristine,

When oceans roar, the hearts beat,

The sky shines & creates feat,

The higher the wave, the higher the scenery,

The oceans stride in pride even without much greenery!

The beauty of life is simplicity,

Sometimes being humble and sometimes being anticity...!

Being… Poetical and mystical,

I often find nature a bit too lyrical!

Lonely roads make awesome adventures,

Reclusive travel makes the best travel ventures,

Cherish life with the exotic nature,

Calm and soothe yourself with its almighty stature!

14. *Snow and Its Antics*

When snow mysteriously disappears,

And greenery suddenly appears,

It seems as if the sadness was overpowered,

Bringing in light as the happiness showered!

Though I wonder, am I the only one with a fetish for snow?

Am I the only one who loves the sun and its glow?

Am I the only one who loves the deadly silence?

And am I the only one who is smitten with nature's valence?

Sati Siroda

Again, as the snow snows on a snow day,

I wander in wonder in every way,

Happy and amused on the streets,

The road is lost; now, I can only see white snow sheets!

After the snow has snowed,

Even the slightest hope powerfully glowed,

Life eventually came to a circle,

I went out to life dashing after beating the cold blue and purple!

Soon, I realised even when life is glum,

Someone sees the rosy plum,

Exclaims fantasised and in awe,

That life amidst the darkness he saw!

All that's left now is snow and fresh memories of snow,

Approaching homecoming has an excellent feeling, though!

Even the glum waved a smile,

As it is not going to return in a while!

And then Christmas came,

Christmas markets marked the beginning frame,

As it snowed, glowed, and roared…

Sati Siroda

Happiness only dropped and poured...!

15. The Teacher Like the Tathagata

The sun and the moon, the stars, and the sky,

The entire Universe answers when someone asks why,

The light that might just be there but still couldn't be found,

That's when a teacher appears to help you count.

The knowledge is there, but the path to it remains unknown,

A teacher advances to clear the path of difficulties so outgrown,

To achieve the goal, when the creative mind lacks patience,

A teacher appears to channelise and create a perfect balance.

In every life aspect, one follows and obeys the knowledgeful,

Like the Tathagata, who, through his teachings, made one's life meaningful,

Everyone on the right path can show someone the light,

Mark their presence and make someone's future bright.

A teacher, indeed, is the one who can show you your reflection,

The truest of all, like the Tathagata, help you in contemplation,

Wisest of all, enlighten you to choose your path and follow,

Kindest of all, will uplift your spirit and help you conquer your sorrow.

16. The Eagle and Its Prey

About to pounce upon something not so known,

Wild and beautiful, the eagle so grown,

Lurks heavily on its prey,

Looks so classy, even with dark shades of grey...!

Climbs above the clouds to surpass the storm,

Picks its feathers and beak to live long,

Vengeful yet so calm,

Lurks like a shadow, yet so warm!

It knows how to dominate with its presence,

Earnest Poetica

Doesn't bother about the chaos and its terrible essence,

Stays in silence and is filled with fighting anima,

Oh, man! What a bird, and what a charisma!

17. *Love is... The Heart's Pain*

Love is…

An ocean of tears,

Mountain of fears,

Beginning of loneliness,

End of jolliness.

Love is…

A desert of broken hearts,

With countless broken parts,

Dying beautiful stars,

Carrying dark and ugly scars.

Love is…

A prepared bed for death,

A life without breath,

A night without moon,

A flower about to die soon.

Love is…

The end of a season,

Hatred without any reason,

A pond filled with poison,

A problem without a solution.

(Hence,) Love is…

Not to be done,

Needs to be forgotten,

To be thrown out of the heart,

To regain yourself part by part.

18. When I lost Dadai!

Tears were rolling down, and I was all alone,

The one I loved, with time, was now gone,

All that was left were the scattered memories,

Now, I stand them in garland, trying to form stories.

I never thought that this day would come,

Amidst the bushes of the world where I lived would be gone,

I stood by the corner, weeping inside my heart,

The one who wiped my tears, the Universe has drifted him apart.

I could not weep, for my tears had departed with him,

All felt arid as the light of love grew grim,

I saw my father in fragments, a sight to witness,

As thus, the heavens unleashed, he could only murmur, "Oh! Precious."

I had always asked so many things from him all year round,

But never said the three words I always wanted to say aloud,

I loved him, I cared for him, and I needed him,

Were the words that are still in my heart, which were meant for him.

My light of hope was shining scarce and dim,

As my soul left with the soul of his,

Now, I have nobody to share my thoughts with,

What is left now are the memories within.

The last glance of his now I have in memory,

Is of a calm angel with a sparkle of glory,

His striking figure, about six feet tall,

Lingers in my mind, standing proud and tall,

Sati Siroda

Like a silhouette in the air, almost nigh,

Giving me a sense that he is still nearby.

His eyes were so calm, and his smile so hearty,

Remains in memory, his personality so gaudy,

Nevertheless, the truth holds such irony,

He exists now and forever, but only in memory.

Today, he's not here, and the future shows no trace,

Yet why does it seem he's in some hidden place?

Why does it feel like one day he'll return,

And once more, will the world on its axis turn!

Why does it seem that one day, when tomorrow comes,

He'll be there on the railway platform to welcome.

Why does it feel that, upon my next visit to his space,

He'll have been eagerly waiting for days for my embrace.

Why it seems that one day history will be repeated,

And death will stand in front of him, wholly defeated,

Why does it seem that whenever I'd need something funny,

He'll again smile and say, "Come on! I'm here, bunny!"

Who'll answer my questions this time?

Fate was so rude to me, but I need to know why.

To whom I'll now call Dadai,

And with whom I'll see the time passing by.

My heart is aching, and my brain is feeling numb,

Sitting amidst the wall of his house, dumb,

There! He used to stand and gaze at me,

There! He used to dine with the family.

Look here! He used to sit and watch TV,

Look there! He used to complete his client's work perfectly in a jiffy,

Look at the car I used to drive with him,

Look at the fish in the aquarium; they are still waiting for the missing.

I saw him leaving, and I'd let him go,

All I could do was to let the time flow,

I know he'll never return,

And the world will, of course, never turn.

Even though the tears, by now, had their way,

Still, he would never be there to wipe them away,

I know, he already passed away yesterday,

He isn't here today, and tomorrow will never come his way.

I've lost him forever, and that's the truth,

Time will heal, and the memories will be there, although,

But that's how we can console ourselves,

But he'll never return, and his photo will be constantly on the shelves.

19. Glimpses of the Past

On that stormy night, I was walking alone,

I looked behind, but there was no one,

My legs were trembling as I passed the firm houses,

I knew all the plants around were dry, and from them hung dry and dead roses.

There was an iron gate standing firm on the earth,

Through which I'd loved to enter since my birth.

But today, my heart was throbbing while I entered,

Because everything had changed and is all now so weird.

What life holds inside is now a surprise,

For someone who has paid the ultimate price.

My wavering steps led me within,

To where lay someone I loved, still in their skin.

I wished for him to stir, but life played its game,

Death enshrouded him, unresponsive to his name.

I crumbled beside his bed in despair and strife,

Struggling to grasp the truth, I lost my senses beside his lifeless life.

My eyes were open, but my lips were numb,

As if my fate suddenly had gone dumb,

I wanted him to know that I wanted him to get up,

That, to stop this game and to wake up.

But the fate was cruel, and I finally gave up,

Cause' I knew he was never going to sit up,

I saw everyone in tears, their hearts shattering,

My lips remained numb while my teeth were chattering.

Four men arrived and took him away,

Beside him, I walked, his cover in my sway.

Sati Siroda

I cried without tears, my grief hard to bear,

Sadness filled the air, as happiness seemed rare.

I reached the place where he was to be kept,

Cold and raining, it was, with pain in every chest.

He feared the cold, yet there we left him alone,

We returned, but my heart could no longer find its home.

In the morning, we rushed back to the place,

I realised there were no white roses to decorate his grave,

Till I returned with the flowers there,

He was already decorated with a lot of care.

I couldn't bear the sight of his departure,

Trembling, yet someone offered capture.

We brought him back to his beloved home,

For his final journey to his eternal dome.

There, everything lay shattered, carelessly arrayed,

All I could do was stare blankly at the disarray displayed.

I couldn't grasp why everyone was crying,

Until someone slapped me, urging tears for the dying.

My dad had asked me not to cry before,

And now my eyes were dry, unable to weep anymore.

Someone screamed while Mom looked worried,

But my pain seemed buried, unable to be hurried.

I'm unsure what followed next,

But I knew I had lost what was once so close and vexed.

We took him to that place where "men meet their fate,"

Waited in line to let him face what lies at that gate.

Fraud! Yes, fraud! What else can fate be named?

Even the prayers before him seemed so outdated, so untamed.

I was seated beside him, holding his crinkled hand,

Trying to find out if there was even a slight sight of his life's band.

But no! He had was long gone to heaven to serve thy beings,

I could have flown to him only if I had wings,

I sat there till he was burnt to ashes,

Knowing nothing, except that he was gone with few fire flashes.

Thereafter, his ashes were immersed in a holy river,

Yet when I recall that day, my hands still quiver.

I know I'll never meet him again; it's plain,

I must live on with my heart and its pain.

The glimpses of this history will forever stay,

Though others may forget, I never shall stray.

All I wish is to have him back once more,

Even though I know this prayer is in vain, to the core...!

20. Miss You

Meantime, when you are not around, I miss you till the moment you're there,

Meantime when you are around, I miss you by thinking about when you will not be here,

I wish I could stop the time so that you could never leave,

But destiny always plays a stupid game in case of need.

The smile you shower on me, the blessed voice you have,

Makes me go crazy and closer to you, more than I ever had,

I don’t have words to express it, nor do I have the guts to show,

All I have is my beating heart that is flowing with your flow.

I wish I could have been with you; I wish the distance could have been a few miles,

So that I can come across any time and wish you with a smile,

Many must have told you that you are very sweet,

But for me, trust me, you are the biggest grand treat.

Life has never been simple, but your innocence is what makes it so,

My heart waved me the signal, “Ready, steady and get set, go!”

I hope my care reaches your heart at the earliest possible time,

And that all my “miss you” catch speed and in your heart chime.

I don’t know what’s wrong or what’s happening to me,

Without you, my days and nights are entirely draining, I see.

I can’t bear this departure anymore,

I wish I could bring my heart to your shore.

21. Wishing My Love a Happy Birthday!

The stars shone down on the very day I met you,

I wasn't sure what you possessed to make me get you,

Before that day, I had remained numb,

But your love struck me, leaving me dumb.

I cherish you more with each passing day,

My love for you continually grows in every way,

I thank fate for giving me such a lovely gift,

Suddenly, it gave my life a happy lift.

Wishing you, my love, a very happy birthday,

May you live long and strong until eternity's destined day.

You have made my life special and memorable,

May every day of yours be equally cherishable.

I don't have words to express my gratitude,

All I can say, my love, is you embody my attitude.

You live within me, and I am entirely yours,

Before this day ends, may happiness fill your doors.

If ever I have done something good and great,

The Universe will grant your wishes, never too late,

I know these words may not perfectly express Costa,

But it all began with writing, and may it forever ride a roller coaster.

I'm sorry if I've ever hurt you, now or before,

Believe me, I've cried over it more often, that's for sure,

All I can say is I love you more than myself,

I try hard to grant you everything alone, but I'm just not an elf.

But dear sweetheart, thank you for being there,

I treasure you more each day; our love is growing layer by layer,

Happy birthday once again, my love,

Let's cherish every moment and be as affectionate as doves.

22. You're Enough

Embrace thyself with love so pure,

For in your heart, beauty does endure.

Let your soul bloom like a rose in spring,

And cherish every part, your flaws, and your being.

In the mirror, you may see imperfections,

But the beauty lies beyond mere reflections.

Your worth cannot be measured in size or shape,

For you are a masterpiece that no one can replicate.

Embrace your curves, your edges, and your scars,

For they tell stories of the battles you've won so far.

You are a warrior, fierce and bold,

And your self-love is worth more than gold.

Let your heart sing, dance, and shine,

Self-love is a journey, not a one-time line.

In moments of doubt, hold your head up high,

And trust that you are enough, just as you are tonight.

23. Emerging from the Wilderness

I disappeared into the wilderness,

to garner strength and protect my tenderness.

Amidst the trees, I found my peace,

and let go of the chaos that wouldn't cease.

I wandered through the wilderness,

finding solace in its emptiness.

With every step, my heart grew strong,

and I knew I could face whatever came along.

Earnest Poetica

Now, I emerge from the wilderness

with newfound strength and fearlessness.

I may be tender, but I'm not weak,

and I'll stand up for what I believe and seek.

24. Silence and Self-Protection

Having no opinion is also an opinion,

But sometimes silence can be a wise decision,

To protect our peace and avoid collision.

If one doesn't judge, nothing will change amidst the millions,

But sometimes it's better to avoid the din,

And focus on our own growth from within.

Silence can be a powerful intuition,

A moment to reflect and make a wise decision,

To choose our battles and maintain our own vision.

So, let us not be quick to make a division,

Sometimes, peace is found in non-participation,

And our silence can be a form of self-protection.

Having no opinion is also an opinion,

A choice to remain quiet, avoid the collision,

But is it really worth- the consequence of inaction?

If one doesn't judge, nothing will change amidst the millions,

Apathy begets complacency, a dangerous condition,

Sometimes, silence can perpetuate oppression with its permission.

So speak up when needed, let your voice be the ignition,

The spark that sets off a chain reaction,

And together we can create a better world with our conviction.

25. *Women Stand Tall and Strong*

In the face of adversity,

Women stand tall and strong,

With resilience and tenacity,

They endure and carry on.

Through trials and tribulations,

They bear the weight with grace,

Their courage and determination,

A shining light in every place.

For they are the pillars of hope,

The embodiment of strength,

Women rise above the scope,

And conquer any length.

Their power is not in physical might,

But in the depths of their soul,

A force that shines bright,

And makes them whole.

With every challenge that they face,

Women rise to the occasion,

Their hearts are full of unwavering grace,

Their spirit is an unbreakable foundation.

For they are the warriors of life,

Fighting battles every day,

Women of strength and might,

Guiding us on our way.

26. Spring: A New Beginning

I looked and looked, and it was already spring,

A world reborn, a new beginning.

The birds chirped along the wind chimes' ring,

A symphony of life, a joyful singing.

The earth awakens, the flowers bloom,

A tapestry of colours, a sweet perfume.

The sun shines brighter, the air feels light,

A perfect day, a pure delight.

The trees are dressed in a vibrant green,

A sight to behold, a wondrous scene.

The world comes alive, a joyful thing,

A celebration of life, a newfound spring.

So let us revel in this glorious day,

And dance along the fields in gay.

For spring has come, a precious thing,

A time of hope, a time of blooming.

27. She's a Womanpreneur

She is life, she is a Womanpreneur,

A force of nature, a rising conqueror.

With strength and grace, she paves her way,

And builds a future as bright as day.

She rises early, she works late,

A tireless spirit, she won't abate.

She faces challenges with a steady hand,

And overcomes them to make a stand.

She builds her empire, she breaks the mould,

A true visionary, she's worth her weight in gold.

She inspires others with her fire and drive,

And shows them that they, too, can thrive.

She's not afraid to take risks or try,

She never gives up; she never says die.

She's a true leader, a true trailblazer, and a Womanpreneur,

And with every step, she soars higher.

So let us honor this remarkable soul,

A true inspiration, a story to be told.

For she is life, she is a Womanpreneur,

And she's changing the world forevermore.

28. *Woman's Leadership*

In a realm where strength and grace align,

A woman's leadership begins to shine.

With wisdom's torch, she lights the way,

Guiding hearts through night to day.

Her voice, a beacon of passion's fire,

Inspiring minds to reach higher.

She nurtures dreams, ignites the spark,

Empowering others to make their mark.

Sati Siroda

With courage as her trusted shield,

She faces challenges, refusing to yield.

A trailblazer on uncharted trails,

Her vision soars and her spirit never fails.

She leads with empathy and compassion's touch,

Uniting hearts, forging bonds as such.

In her hands, unity finds its space,

As she embraces diversity's grace.

Her resilience in times of strife,

Uplifts her tribe, breathing hope to life.

A leader, fierce yet filled with care,

She builds bridges where love can be shared.

In her footsteps, a legacy blooms,

A testament to the strength that forever looms.

A woman's leadership, a gift untold,

Transforming the world, a story unfolds.

29. *Sarcasm's Charm*

~ A Polite Path to Peace

In times when anger's flame may rise,

Consider wit that's worldly-wise.

When wrath engulfs, be sly and clever,

Sarcasm's touch, a tongue's endeavour.

Forsooth, it slays and aptly fits,

A blade of words, where humour sits.

Amidst the storm, let jest befriend,

A gentle way to heal and mend.

Earnest Poetica

Though ire may tug at the heart's own strings,

With amusing words, new solace springs.

In mirthful tones, let anger cease,

A polished gem, the art of peace.

So when frustration's waves draw near,

Embrace the quip, release the jeer.

For sarcasm wielded with grace,

Brings smiles and laughter in its chase.

In gracious English, let us compose,

With polite poetry, our verses disclose.

Sati Siroda

When fury's grasp, your spirit ensnares,

Embrace sarcasm, for it aptly cares.

When anger's flames do wildly ignite,

Let wit and jest become your might!

Trust my words, dear soul, for they ring true,

Sarcasm's prowess, it indeed shall imbue.

It slays not with harm but with subtle art,

Fitting your bill mends the heart.

With razor-sharp words, it dances and twills,

A gentle weapon that destiny fulfils.

So, when the tempest of rage draws near,

Refrain from wrath; let sarcasm appear.

For in its embrace, serenity thrives,

A powerful balm, as harmony arrives.

30. My Happy Place

In my happy place, a world serene,

Where your presence brings a joy unseen.

It's you, yes, it has always been you,

Your arms, your charms, like morning dew.

Underneath a sky of tranquil blue,

We dance amidst dreams, just us two.

In your embrace, worries dissolve,

A refuge where my heart evolves.

31. Eternal Flame Ignites

In shadows deep, where darkness reigned,

I wandered lost, my spirit pained.

But then, a flicker caught my sight,

A glimmering beacon, pure and bright.

I saw the light shining bright,

Its radiant glow is a guiding light.

With weary limbs and wounded soul,

I pushed my bruised self and stood upright.

Sati Siroda

No longer chained to the endless night,

I found the strength to take my flight.

With each step I took, the light grew near,

Banishing doubts, erasing fear.

In its embrace, I found my way,

A path that led to a brand-new day.

The scars I bore, a testament to true,

To the resilience that pulled me through.

Even in the darkest hour,

When life's storms unleash all their power,

There's hope that shines, a steadfast flame,

Dispelling shadows, erasing shame.

So let us cherish this precious sight,

The light that breaks through the darkest night.

With renewed vigour, we'll rise and fight,

And push ourselves to stand upright.

Through life's chaos and ceaseless strife,

You're the sanctuary, my anchor for life.

In your eyes, a flicker of pure delight,

Guiding me through both day and night.

Sati Siroda

With your smile, the sun begins to rise,

Painting the horizon with vibrant dyes.

Your laughter, a melody that fills the air,

Banishing darkness, chasing away despair.

My happy place is where we reside,

A haven where love and dreams collide.

Together, we create a world so true,

Enveloped in the warmth of me and you.

So here, in this realm of endless grace,

I find solace in a smiling face.

It's you, forever my heart's sweetest tune,

In my happy place, forever immune.

32. *Whispers of Tranquility*

Sitting in tranquility with a cup of coffee,

Time passed swiftly as I hurried along.

Embracing myself, I witnessed in the coffee's haze,

Even the sky had dimmed gradually as I rushed ahead.

But now, at this moment, I find solace anew,

As I immerse myself in nature's vibrant hue.

The bustling world fades, its noise becomes still,

Revealing a serene landscape, calm and tranquil.

The sun peeks through the canopy of trees,

Casting a golden glow on the dancing leaves.

Birds sing their melodies, sweet and clear,

Their songs of freedom, devoid of any fear.

A gentle breeze whispers through the tall grass,

Caressing my face with a tender caress.

The fragrance of flowers fills the air,

A symphony of scents beyond any compare.

I gaze upon a meandering stream,

Its waters reflect the sun's gentle beam.

A symphony of colours, a painter's delight,

Sati Siroda

Nature's masterpiece, a breathtaking sight.

The mountains stand tall, majestic, and grand,

Their peaks reaching for the heavens, unplanned.

Snow-capped and regal, they inspire awe,

A testament to nature's boundless flaw.

In this moment, I let go of my worries and strife,

Immersed in the serenity of nature's embrace.

I find peace within, a stillness deep,

As nature whispers its secrets, secrets it'll keep.

The rhythm of life slows down to a crawl,

As I surrender to nature's beckoning call.

Time becomes irrelevant; it loses its grip,

As I find harmony in this tranquil trip.

So, I sit here, content with my cup of coffee,

In the lap of nature, I find my serenity.

Grateful for this respite, this moment of grace,

I'll cherish it always, in my heart's sacred space.

33. The Unyielding Light

The courage never failed me,

Bright sunshine or darkest nights, it had always trailed me,

Through the storms and calm, it guided my sail,

In moments of doubt, it was my unbreakable rail.

In the echoes of silence, it was my voice,

Giving me strength, in despair, a choice,

Against the tides of fear, a formidable shield,

In life's vast battlefield, my unwavering yield.

Through every fall and rise, a constant beam,

Transforming every nightmare into a dream,

In courage, I found a friend so true,

A force within, in every hue.

In every step, with courage, I tread,

A path of hope, by its light, I am led,

With courage in heart, nothing seems frail,

For in its embrace, I set my sail.

34. The Waiting Game

Waiting is a game I don't want to play,

It steals the colours, leaving skies grey,

In the halls of time echoes my silent plea,

For moments lost, and what could be.

The clock ticks on, relentless and sly,

As dreams in the shadows quietly lie,

Yet in this waiting, a lesson so stark,

Patience, sometimes, ignites a spark.

With every second, hope intertwines,

In the slow dance of the passing times,

Waiting, a teacher in a silent guise,

Unveiling truths hidden from the eyes.

Though waiting feels like a lingering stay,

It moulds the soul in an unseen way,

In 'The Art of Living,' a subtle play,

Transforming nights into a brighter day.

35. The Path of Loving Kindness

Loving-kindness is the way to life,

A remedy for strife, a shield in strife,

It heals the wounds of heart and mind,

Guiding us to a more compassionate goal, entirely determined.

In gentle words and tender touch,

It gives so little yet means so much,

A light in the darkness, a guide so bright,

Turning wrongs into gentle rights.

Through acts of love, big or small,

It breaks down walls, helps us stand tall,

In kindness, we find a powerful key,

Unlocking a world where we all are free.

Loving-kindness, a simple, profound choice,

In its melody, the heart finds its voice,

A journey through both day and night,

In kindness, we find life’s most extraordinary light.

With every act of kindness shown,

Wounds of the mind begin to atone,

The gentle touch, the empathetic ear,

In loving kindness, our doubts disappear.

It soothes the ache of a troubled mind,

Leaving peace and solace behind,

In the warmth of a compassionate embrace,

The mind finds its rightful place.

Through loving-kindness, we find release,

From burdens that once refused to cease,

A balm for wounds that time can't heal,

In its embrace, the mind finds its zeal.

36. *Shades of Humanity*

I wasn't brown, my skin was,

Yet worth wasn't determined by hue but by cause,

In the tapestry of life, colours blend,

In the end, it's the heart that we defend.

Race didn't determine my worth, but the pain did,

In the crucible of suffering, our souls amid,

For every tear shed, a story untold,

In the depths of our struggle, we unfold.

Sati Siroda

In the face of adversity, we find our might,

Breaking barriers, reaching for the light,

For beneath the surface, we're all the same,

In the heart of humanity, we find our flame.

So let us rise above the divides that bind,

Embrace the beauty of the humankind,

For in unity, our strength is found,

In the symphony of voices, love resound.

Together, we stand, hand in hand,

In solidarity, we make our stand,

For, in the end, it's not the colour of skin,

But the depth of our souls that we let in.

37. Homeward Bound

I long to go back home,

To stay in peace in the place I love, never to roam,

In the warmth of its embrace, find solace true,

With love surrounding me, like morning dew.

The journey back, a winding road,

But in its arms, I find my abode,

For home is not just walls and roof,

It's where love resides, eternal and aloof.

In its presence, I find my song,

Earnest Poetica

In its essence, I feel I belong,

For the love is the anchor, strong and steady,

In its embrace, I find my sanctuary ready.

So let me journey back to where I'm known,

To stay in peace with love, never to be alone,

For in its passion, I find my worth,

Homebound, I return to the place of my hearth.

38. Embracing the Present

In the haze of what's gone by, I'm lost,

But in the present, I pay no cost,

I'm here, in this moment, with no fear,

Believing in its goodness, ever clear.

The path ahead, winding and unknown,

But in this now, I'm not alone,

With each step I take, a tale unfurls,

In life's tapestry, it twists and twirls.

The souls I encounter on this journey's track,

Their kindness leaves an indelible mark,

Though they may be just a step away,

Their goodness brightens my day.

In the embrace of the present, I find my sanctuary,

A refuge from regrets and worries, a place to be free,

For it's here, in the now, where life truly unfolds,

Where joy resides and the future moulds.

No longer bound by what's behind or what's to come,

I savour each moment like the beat of a drum,

For in the present lies the power to create,

To shape my destiny, to choose my fate.

Here, I find the essence of life's sweetest gifts,

In the laughter of loved ones, in the sun as it shifts,

In the simple pleasures that make life worthwhile,

In the beauty of each fleeting smile.

39. *Lessons of Light*

The moon taught me to be calm,

In its gentle glow, I found a soothing balm,

With its serene light, it whispered peace,

In the darkness, my worries would cease.

The sun taught me to rise and shine,

To embrace each day, to make it mine,

With its golden rays, it kissed the sky,

In its warmth, I felt alive, oh so high.

Sati Siroda

From the moon and sun, I learned,

In their wisdom, my spirit yearned,

To find balance in the ebb and flow,

In the light and dark, to let my soul grow.

So let me heed the lessons of light,

In the calm of the moon and the sun so bright,

For in their guidance, I find my way,

To shine my brightest each and every day.

40. Ode to Books

The books give me the pleasure that I long for,

In their pages, I find a boundless store,

Of worlds unknown, waiting to explore,

My only treasure, leaving me wanting more.

They are my solace in times of strife,

In their embrace, I find my life,

Each word is a gift, a balm for my soul,

In their stories, I find myself whole.

Sati Siroda

Through the pages, I escape reality's grip,

Into realms of fantasy, I let my mind slip,

With every sentence, a new adventure begins,

In the world of books, my spirit sings.

So, I immerse myself in their embrace,

In the comfort of their familiar grace,

For in their pages, I find my sanctuary,

My cherished treasure, my literary treasury.

Their words weave a tapestry of dreams,

A symphony of thoughts, flowing in streams,

With each turn of the page, I'm transported afar,

To lands unknown, beneath the sun and star.

In the silence of the night, they whisper tales,

Of heroes and heroines, of ships with sails,

Of love and loss, of triumph and despair,

In their stories, I find refuge from life's glare.

They are my companions through thick and thin,

In their presence, I find peace within,

For within their covers, I find a friend,

Whose company I'll cherish till the end.

So I lose myself in their embrace,

In the magic of their eternal grace,

For in the world of books, I am free,

My heart, my mind, forever wandering, untamed and carefree.

41. Embracing Eternity

Life, death, age, and sickness are universal,

Live the moment; what you have is so personal.

In each heartbeat, find a timeless rehearsal,

For in fleeting breaths, we craft the immortal.

Moments fleeting, like whispers in the nocturnal,

Each second is a treasure in the grand life's journal.

Embrace the dance, both joyous and formal,

In life's grand play, we are but actors eternal.

Sati Siroda

Under the sun, each day, so diurnal,

Our souls speak in colours, bright and infernal.

Hold close to love, so profoundly paternal,

In the vast cosmos, our stories are celestial.

Life's journey, complex and yet so kernel,

In the face of time, stand strong and fraternal.

For in each ending, there's a start, vernal,

In life and death, find lessons, eternal.

42. The Symphony of Breath

Breathe, breathe, just breathe,

Every breath is precious, a life's sheath.

Inhale courage, exhale grief, weave

Through life's maze, with each breath, believe.

In the whispers of the wind, bequeath,

Dreams and hopes, like autumn leaves beneath.

For in each breath lies a story, a wreath,

Of moments, memories, a silent heath.

Sati Siroda

With each breath, let your soul unsheathe,

Embrace life's colours from underneath.

In every gasp, life's essence we wreathe,

A tale of resilience with each breath we breathe.

As tempests rage and storms of life seethe,

Breathe calmly, find peace, like a sword in its sheathe.

In tranquillity, our anxious thoughts wreath,

With each gentle breath, we rise from beneath.

Calm breathing, like a serene lake, bequeath,

Clarity and strength, an unseen sheath.

In its rhythm, our worries unweave,

Harmony is restored; in calm breaths, we breathe.

So in moments of turmoil, when we seethe,

Remember the power of a calm breath's heath.

For in each steady inhale and exhale, bequeath

A beacon of hope, in calm breaths, we weave.

43. Triumph in Tears

The day you laughed through tears,

It was the day you won over fears.

At that moment, so sincere,

Life's beauty became crystal clear.

With every chuckle, doubts disappear,

In your eyes, a new frontier.

Strength found in joyous jeers,

Turning sorrow into a triumphant cheer.

In laughter, hope engineers,

A fortress against life's spears.

In joy, the heart steers,

Through storms, a path it shears.

So laugh through the tears, my dears,

Embrace each challenge that nears.

For in laughter, life endears,

A journey of love through the years.

44. Lessons in the Journey

There are a whole lot of lessons to learn by thyself,

Between tripping and catching yourself.

The world so serene hits rock bottom when you trip,

And the sail gets adjusted; you soar far the moment you get a grip.

In the stumble, there's wisdom, a deep wellspring,

Where failure and triumph together cling.

Each fall, a heartbreak, a story, a lesson to equip,

In the art of living, each slip is a wonderful script.

As you rise, like a phoenix from the deep,

The lessons you've learned are yours to keep.

In resilience, you'll find a powerful fellowship,

With yourself and your mind in each recovery's leap.

So, embrace each tumble and every slip,

In these moments, the character is chiselled and chipped.

Life's journey, a sea where we all ship,

In learning, in growing, let your heart equip.

45. Kaizen

~ The Path of Continuous Growth

Kaizen your life, your each step, and your mind,

Kaizen isn't only for your workspace but for you to follow it everywhere,

A philosophy not just for the grind,

But a beacon to guide, to be fair and square.

In each action lies a chance to refine,

A pursuit of improvement in all that you bear.

It's not just in work but in how you dine,

In how you speak, listen, love, and care.

This journey of growth, a constant align,

With values and goals, in the air you breathe, rare.

In every small step, let your light shine,

Kaizen is a path of progress beyond compare.

In the spirit of kaizen, let yourself entwine,

With a lifelong quest, an unending affair.

In each moment, a possibility divine,

To enhance, to enrich, to become aware.

46. The Silent Witness

The notebook by my bedside didn't tell my age,

But the pages knew how old were the dates,

In every line, a silent sage,

Each word is a memory that resonates.

In ink, emotions engage,

Stories of joy, love, and heartaches.

The scribbles on each page, a backstage,

To a life's play, with its retakes.

As seasons change from the youthful stage,

Earnest Poetica

To years when time accelerates,

This notebook is more than just a cage,

Of thoughts, a companion that navigates.

Though silent, it's a wise mage,

A testament to my life's debates.

In its embrace, wisdoms wage,

A journey through my life's intricate gates.

As I closed thee notebook after writing tonight,

I looked at the stars shining bright,

I have indeed lived a happy life,

Sati Siroda

A triumphant life of wisdom and strife.

In each star, I found a story alight,

Echoes of laughter, love, and slight.

In their glow, a guiding light,

Leading through many a dark night.

My notebook, a reflection quite,

Of a journey through day and night.

In its pages, my heart's kite,

Soaring, dipping in emotional flight.

This life of mine, a tapestry tight,

Woven with threads of dark and light.

In its fabric, an endless sight,

Of love, loss, joy, and twilight.

47. The Paradox of Desire

In soaring summer, we wanted snow,

In freezing winters, we wanted the heat to flow,

We always want what we don't have.

Never happy with something to combat.

Like chasing shadows, a ceaseless show,

In pursuit of the unknown, to and fro.

In our desires, a constant scat,

We yearn for what's not in our habitat.

In spring's bloom, we long for autumn's glow,

In vibrant cities, for quiet meadows low.

The grass seems greener, a well-known spat,

In another's field, we lay our hat.

Yet, amidst this chase, wisdom can grow,

To appreciate our now, not the status quo.

In contentment, find where happiness is at,

In what we have, not in what we combat.

48. Echoes of Silence and Solitude

Silence... is it eerie, peaceful, or anxious?

Solitude... is it perfect, lonely, or obnoxious?

In quietude's embrace, feelings so spacious,

A realm where thoughts can be both audacious and gracious.

In silence, a canvas, neither black nor spacious,

A mirror reflecting our inner chorus or raucous.

In solitude, a journey, sometimes vivacious,

Other times, a path inward, curious, and capacious.

Each silent moment, a question, not vexatious,

A chance to listen to the heart, so sagacious.

Solitude, an invitation, not always audacious,

But a moment for the mind to be tenacious.

In the quiet, find wisdom, not audacious,

In solitude, discover strength, not precarious.

For in both lies a world so spacious and gracious,

A universe within, both tranquil and audacious.

49. In the Depths of Darkness

The shades of black, still, and deep,

Absorb and retain the stains complete.

In its embrace, the secrets it keeps,

A canvas for the night, so discreet.

Like a quiet ocean, vast and steep,

It cradles our fears in its fleet.

Yet in its darkness, stars peep,

Guiding lights, their promises replete.

In black's depth, emotions seep,

A refuge where heart and shadow meet.

In its silence, wisdoms leap,

Lessons of resilience, bitter and sweet.

So, in the darkest hour, don't weep,

For even in black, hope does not deplete.

In its depths, there lies a beauty, not bleak,

A symphony of life, profound and replete.

In the night when blacks soar high,

It engulfs, roars, and flies,

A cloak of mystery in the sky,

Under which the whole world lies.

This hue, in its infinite sprawl,

It holds the universe, vast and tall.

In its depths, stars gallantly call,

A cosmic dance that mesmerises us all.

Black, a colour of power and might,

In its embrace, one finds the night.

A canvas for dreams, taking flight,

In its richness, we find insight.

So, in the embrace of the dark, don’t shy,

For in black, truth and beauty lie.

In its depths, our spirits can fly,

Black remains a colour, both humble and high.

50. The Inner Journey

Rest in peace, Oh dear mind,

Believe that sometimes there is nothing to find,

A step inside is where the journey must go,

Breathe in, breathe out, and just let the breath flow.

In this quiet, let your thoughts unwind,

In the silence of mind, a sanctuary designed.

Where worries dissolve, like melting snow,

In the rhythm of breathing, find your glow.

In this inner world, be both calm and kind,

To the chaos outside, be deaf and blind.

Let the inner peace, like a river, grow,

Nurture it gently; let it quietly bestow.

So rest, dear mind, in this retreat, you'll find,

A haven of calm, for your spirit aligned.

In this journey within, let your true self show,

In the simplicity of solitude, let your wisdom flow.

Thank You

Hey there, thank you for making it to the end—cheers to that!

I'm so glad we got to share this journey. I hope it left you with fresh insights, a little inspiration, and a new way of seeing the small moments that matter. If you enjoyed the read, I'd love it if you left a quick review. Just a few words can go a long way in helping me create more stories—the kind that help you notice the little things or guide you toward the beauty of life.

SCAN ME

>> Leave a Review on Amazon<<

Thanks for being a part of this. Seriously, you're the best!

About the Author

Sati Siroda is an inspirational author passionate about empowering young minds through storytelling. With a knack for weaving simple yet profound tales, Sati inspires readers to embrace their unique potential and navigate life with courage and purpose.

Sati's diverse academic journey—from engineering to education, business, and communication—combined with her extensive travels and time spent in various countries for education, business, and skill development, shapes her holistic storytelling approach. Her experience teaching in schools and universities has further enriched her understanding of young minds, helping her find her path as a storyteller who connects deeply with her audience. Her multifaceted background enables her to connect with readers in relatable and innovative ways.

Her stories are fueled by a belief in the transformative power of narrative. Drawing from her expertise in strategic communication and her love for literature, Sati crafts engaging, uplifting books that instill resilience, emotional intelligence, and self-confidence in her readers. Her mission is clear: to inspire the next generation to dream fearlessly, think critically, and approach life's challenges with creativity and optimism.

Through her heartfelt stories, Sati creates a world where every page becomes a stepping stone toward growth, and every character serves as a guiding light. She warmly invites readers of all ages to embark on a journey of self-love, self-discovery, and empowerment through the enchantment of her books.

Stay connected with Sati Siroda on Instagram: ***@SatiSiroda***.

www.ingramcontent.com/pod-product-compliance
Ingram Content Group UK Ltd.
Pitfield, Milton Keynes, MK11 3LW, UK
UKHW021400190726
13845UKWH00028B/787

9 788196 645847